WAY TO GO

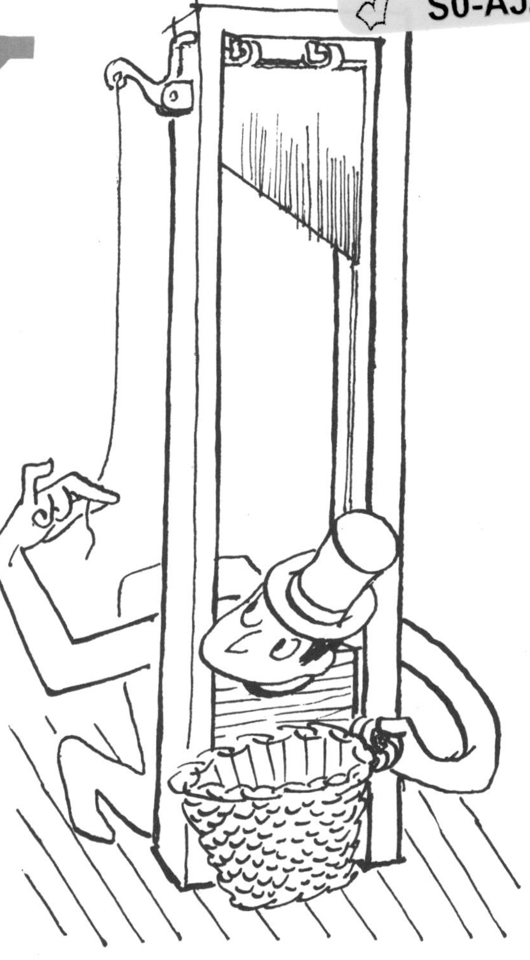

HARRY MAYEROVITCH

DRAWN AND QUARTERLY
D&Q

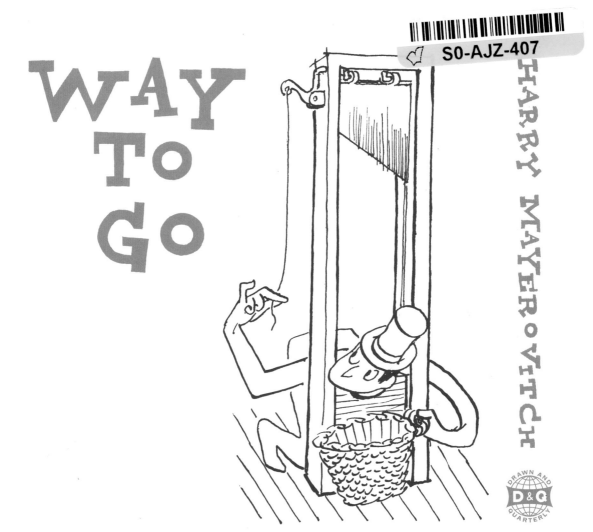

By the same author:

- Overstreet: An Urban Street Development System (1973)
- The Other One: A Book Of Satirical Drawings (1973)
- 20 Drawings: A Portfolio Of Drawings From The Model (1973)
- Once Over Lightly: A Book Of Verses (1973)
- Jibes, Jabs & Jeers: A Book Of Political Cartoons And Verses (1987)
- The Second Coming: A Book Of Cartoons (1993)
- Kaput: A Book Of Cartoons (1993)
- How Architecture Speaks: The Buildings We Make and the Lives We Lead (1996)
- Bernie: A Book Of Cartoons (2000)

Part of the work in this book was originally published in the book *The Other One* (Harvest House, 1973) and excerpts have been published in *Drawn & Quarterly* Volume 3 (2000) and Volume 5 (2003).

Design: Steven Guarnaccia and Chris Oliveros. Cover type: Steven Guarnaccia. Publisher: Chris Oliveros. Publicity: Peggy Burns.

Drawn & Quarterly
Post Office Box 48056
Montreal, Quebec
Canada H2V 4S8
www.drawnandquarterly.com

National Library of Canada Cataloguing in Publication
Mayerovitch, Harry, 1910—
Way To Go / Harry Mayerovitch; introduction by Steven Guarnaccia.
ISBN 1-896597-82-3
1. Canadian wit and humour, Pictorial. I. Title.
NC1449.M39A3 2004 741.5'971 C2004-900844-7

First edition: April 2004. Printed in Hong Kong.
10 9 8 7 6 5 4 3 2 1

The publisher gratefully acknowledges The Canada Council for The Arts for its support of this edition.

Distributed in the USA by:
Chronicle Books
85 Second Street
San Francisco, CA. 94105
800.722.6657

Distributed in Canada by:
Raincoast Books
9050 Shaughnessy Street
Vancouver, BC V6P 6E5
800.663.5714

For Betty Anne

Introduction
by Steven Guarnaccia

An object's shadow, like that cast on the wall of Plato's cave, is often mistaken for the object itself. In photographic experiments made in the 1920s by Dr. Paul Wolff, among other photographers, we sometimes are made to wonder if it's not the shadow that casts the three-dimensional form, if the body itself isn't a product of the shadow, rather than the other way around.

Shadows make ideal subject matter for artists, especially those artists whose work is essentially flat, and makes no effort to create the illusion of three-dimensionality. It goes without saying that a shadow is best rendered in black and white, and doesn't need color to effectively portray it. A shadow's closest kin may be the inkblot. In fact, the Phantom Blot, one of Mickey Mouse's nemeses in the classic strips drawn by Floyd Gottfredson, is little more than a shadow that has picked itself up, unhitched itself from the body that cast it, and run off to raise terror.

There is something uncanny about shadows—they suggest both a presence and an absence. They are like dark ghosts that seem to have a life of their own, but are inextricably tied to the living. They frighten us when they slither along the contours of a wall, when they loom larger than the figure they're attached to, when we stare into the bottomlessness of the void that they represent—but they comfort as well. Their presence reassures us of our corporeality, of our very existence. For what is it that casts no shadow, but the dead, or worse, the undead?

Harry Mayerovitch's drawings of shadows, collected in his book of 1973, *The Other One,* are impish and pixilated. Like Peter Pan's shadow, they struggle for lives of their own. But unlike Peter's shadow, they lead their autonomous lives without detaching themselves from their masters—they need no needle and thread to remain connected. In fact, their mischief is best made in close proximity to their makers, the better to mock them. There's the shadow that gives its body a hotfoot and the one that rears back to launch a snowball at its body's top hat. The shadow cast by one man even dares to take the form of a woman. These are no mere shadow puppets that merely mimic their makers.

Below: drawing for the dedication of the 1973 edition of The Other One: *"Reverently dedicated to myself, without whose unflagging efforts, infinite patience, and unbridled vanity this book could not have emerged from the shadows."*

Mayerovitch keeps company with other artists who have played shadow games. There is J.J. Grandville, whose book *Un Autre Monde* featured shadows behaving in unexpected ways. Sergio Aragones had another take on the theme in his long running feature in *Mad,* "The Shadow Knows." The shadow is a device I return to continually as an artist. When I add a shadow to a figure it grounds the figure in the landscape, and immediately creates a sense of depth in the drawing. When I want to comment on a human situation, I often turn to a shadow as a kind of Greek chorus of one that has the same relationship to the figure in a drawing as the black-clad puppeteer has to his Bunraku puppet. It's a presence that suggests that there may exist another dimension beyond the third.

I was first introduced to Harry Mayerovitch's shadow drawings in *Drawn & Quarterly* Volume 3. I was immediately taken with their crisp, witty line. They seemed utterly contemporary, but they had a timeless quality about them that made me think that they might be from any decade. I was delighted to learn that they were made not in the 1950s or the 1990s, but in the graphically undistinguished 1970s.

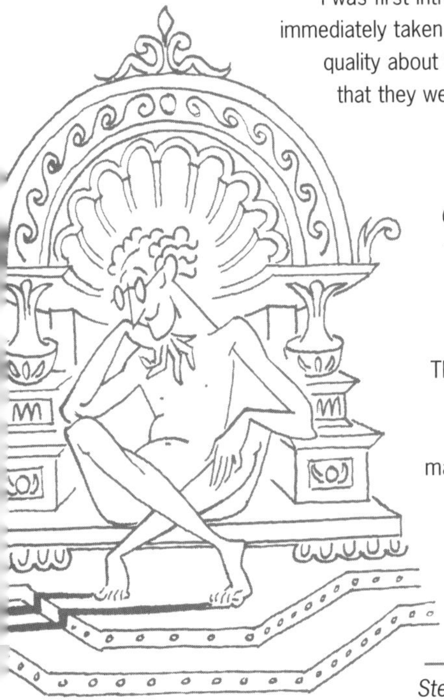

The drawings from *The Other One* comprise over half of the work seen here. But there are gems from Mayerovitch's collection of drawings about death called *Way To Go,* as well as drawings from his sketchbooks. The sketchbook drawings reveal a gentler, more poignant vision than that of either the wiseguy sass of the images from *The Other One,* or the morbidly mordant drawings about ending it all found in *Way to Go.*

The drawings about death are from the latest period of Mayerovitch's creative life. These are not the idle musings of a young man for whom death is a far-off abstraction, but the close-to-the-bone drawings of someone who is eyeball to eyeball with his subject matter. In this respect they recall Warren Zevon's last recordings about mortality made while he was dying, or the daily drawings James Flora made at the end of his life, hooked up to a respirator and fully aware that he was putting his last lines on paper.

Taken together, these drawings suggest an artist of many parts, one with a consistency of wit and point of view. And they confirm that each of these many parts has a life of its own that together add up to one coherent creative personality.

Steven Guarnaccia is an artist and is the art director of The New York Times *Op-Ed page.*

The Other One

"No, no! I am but shadow of myself;
You are deceived, my substance is not here."
— William Shakespeare

"Follow a shadow, it still flies you,
Seem to fly it, it will pursue."
—Ben Jonson

"Still nursing the unconquerable hope,
Still clutching the inviolable shade."
—Matthew Arnold

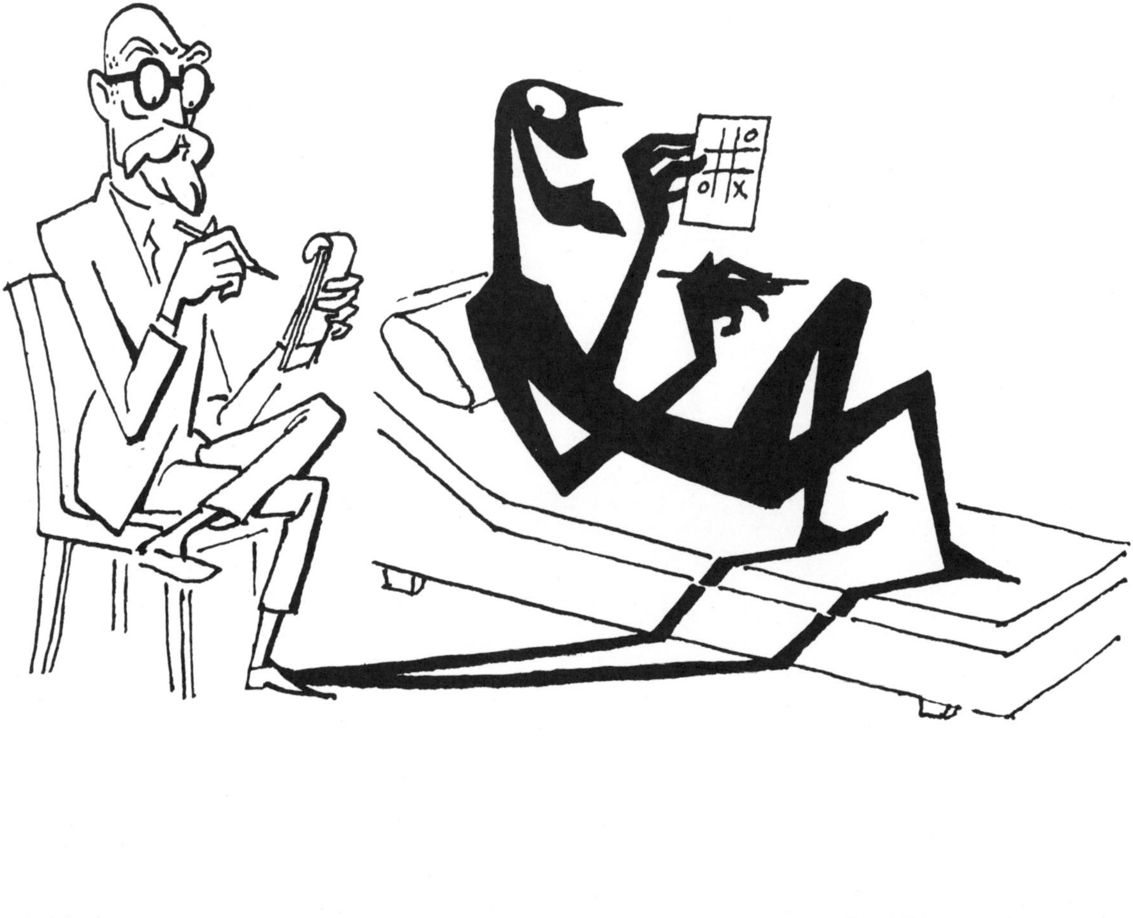

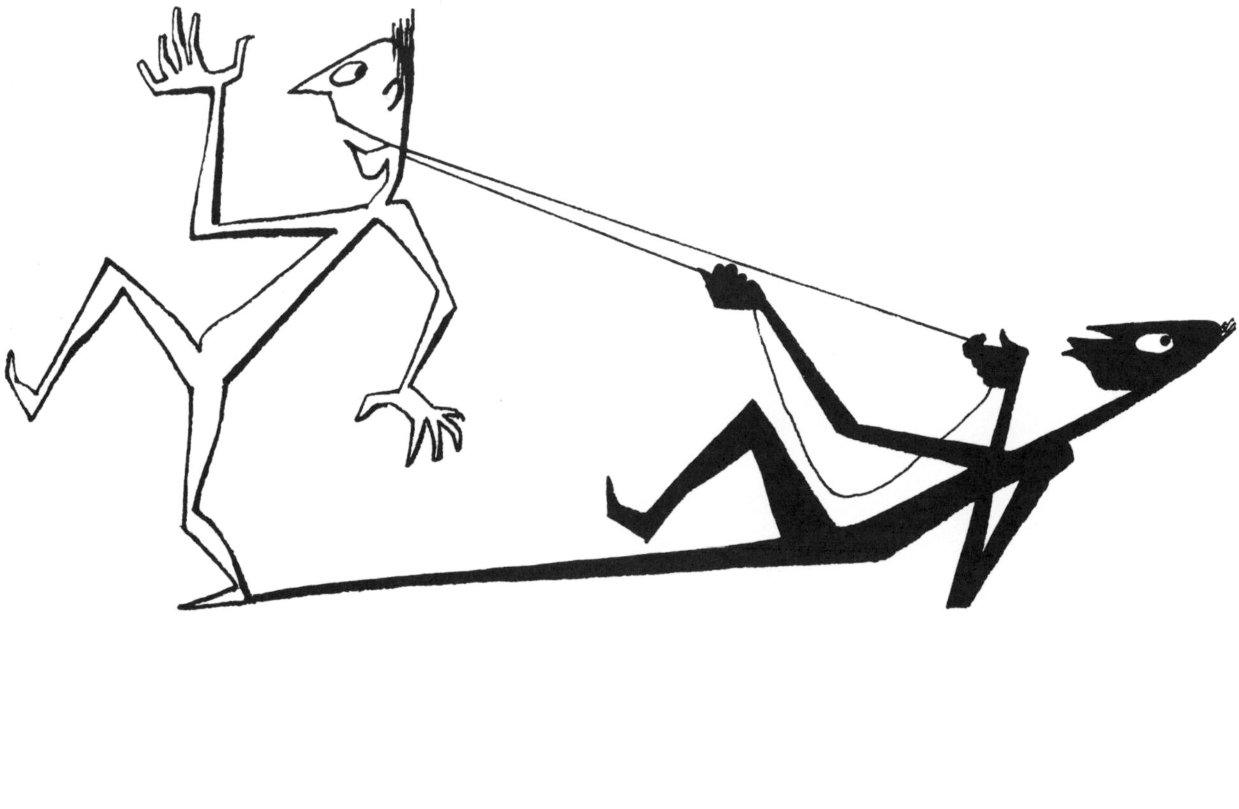

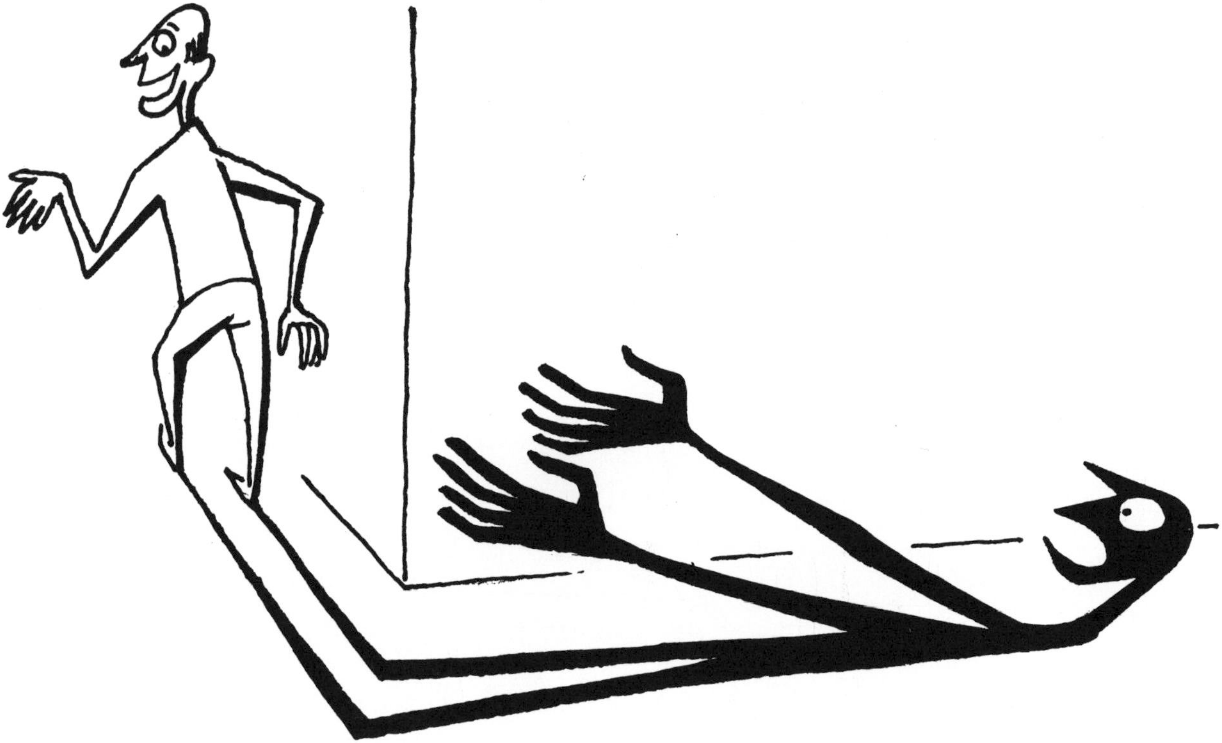

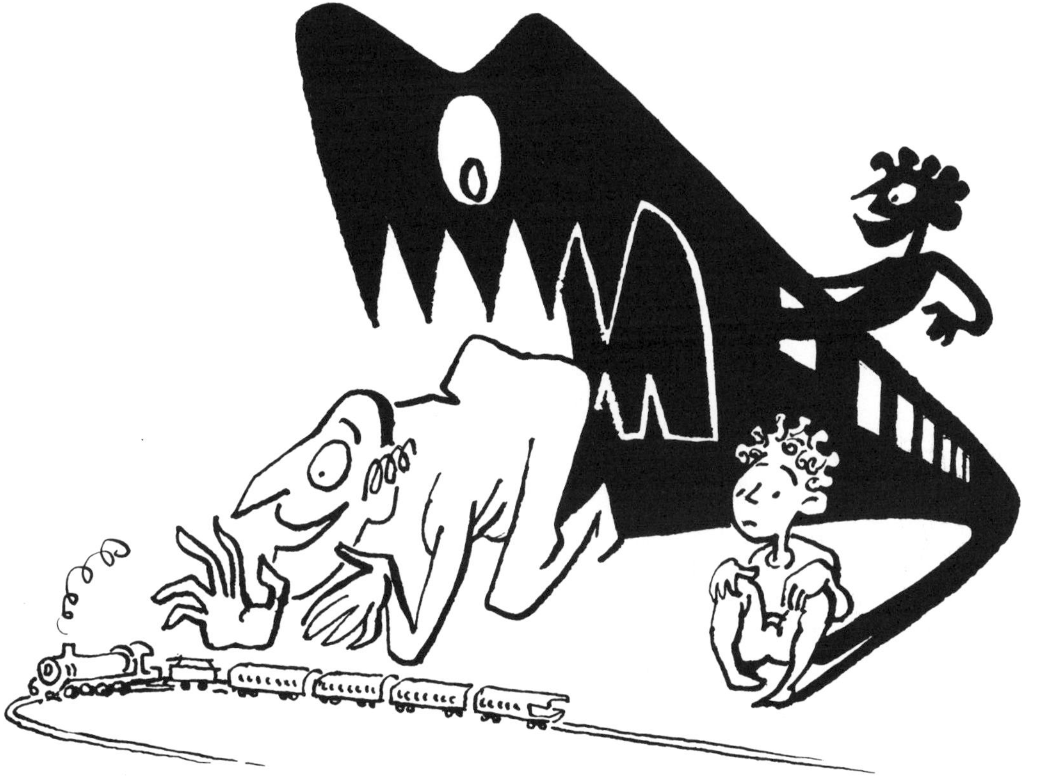

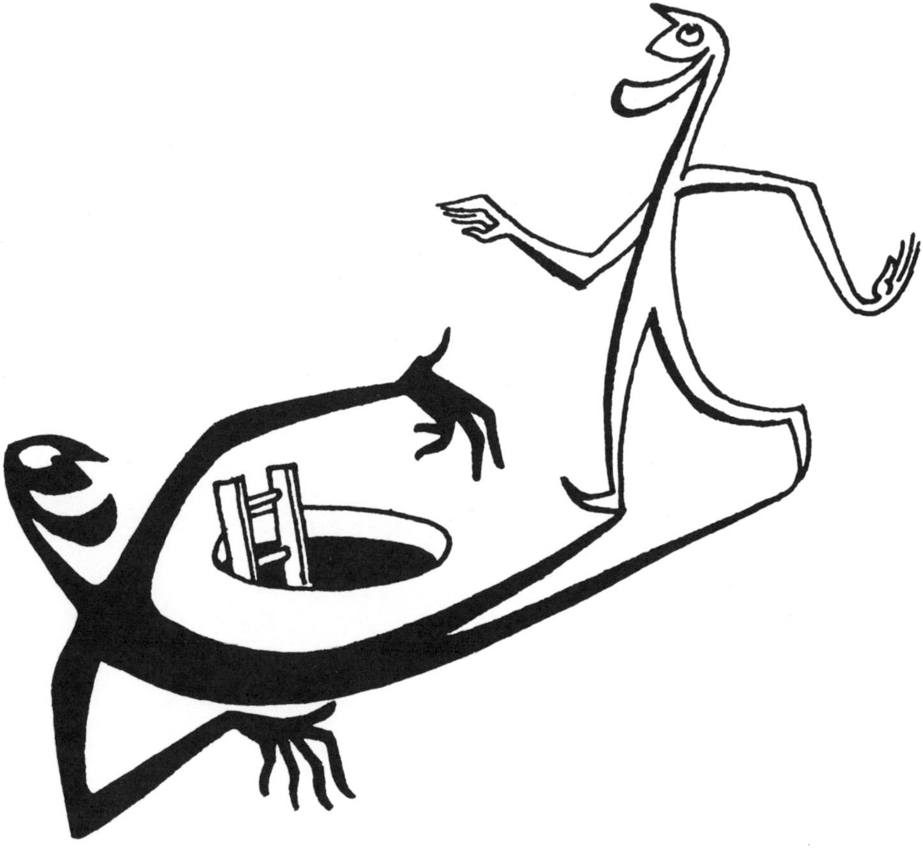

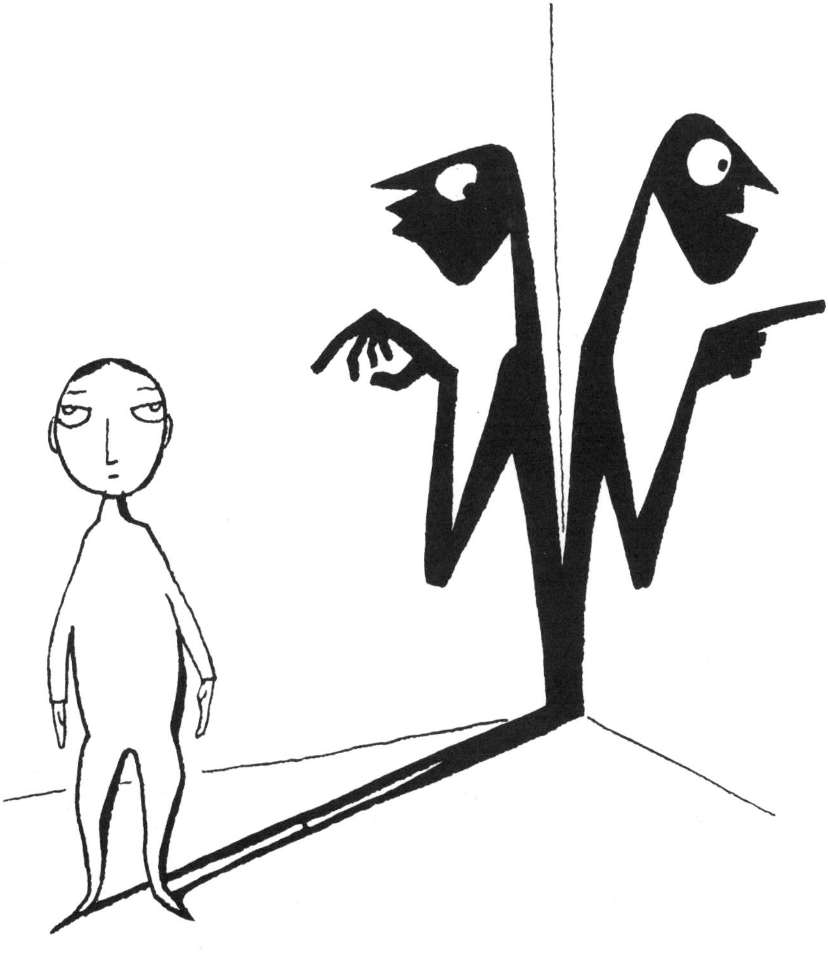

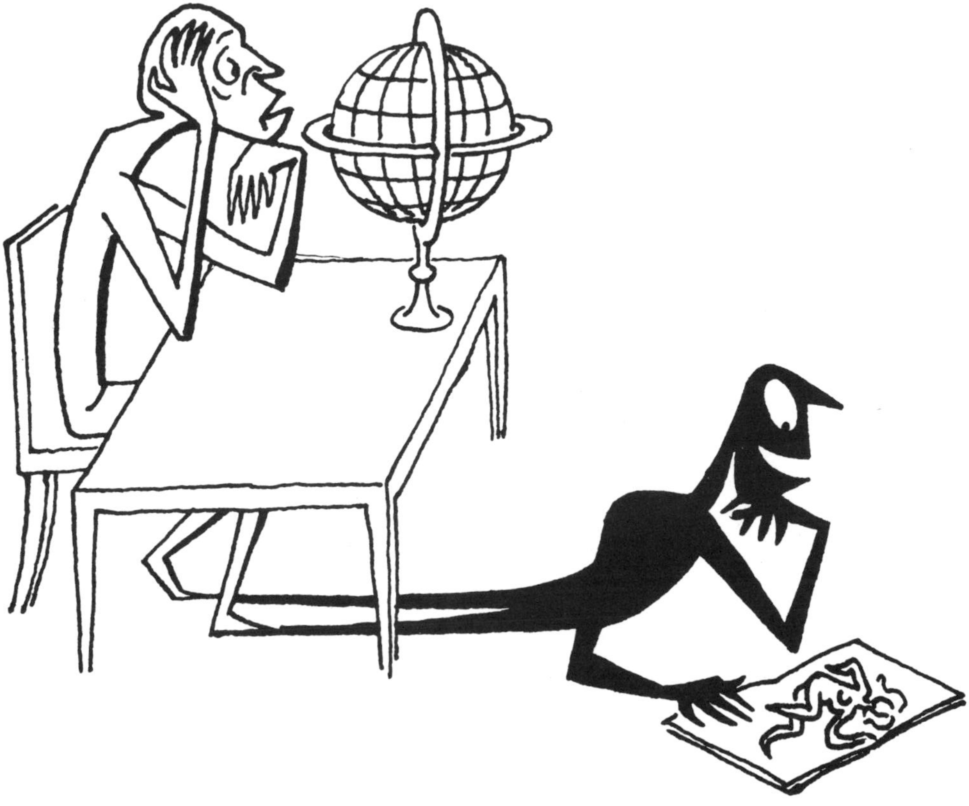

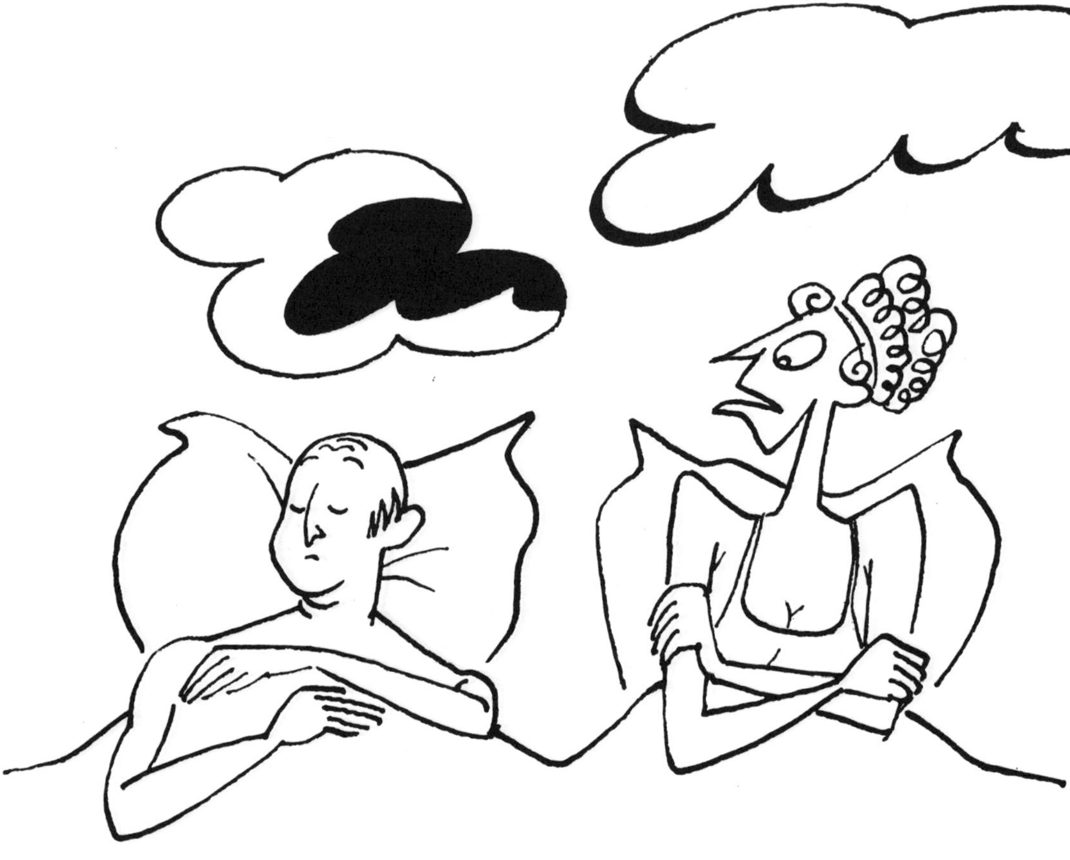

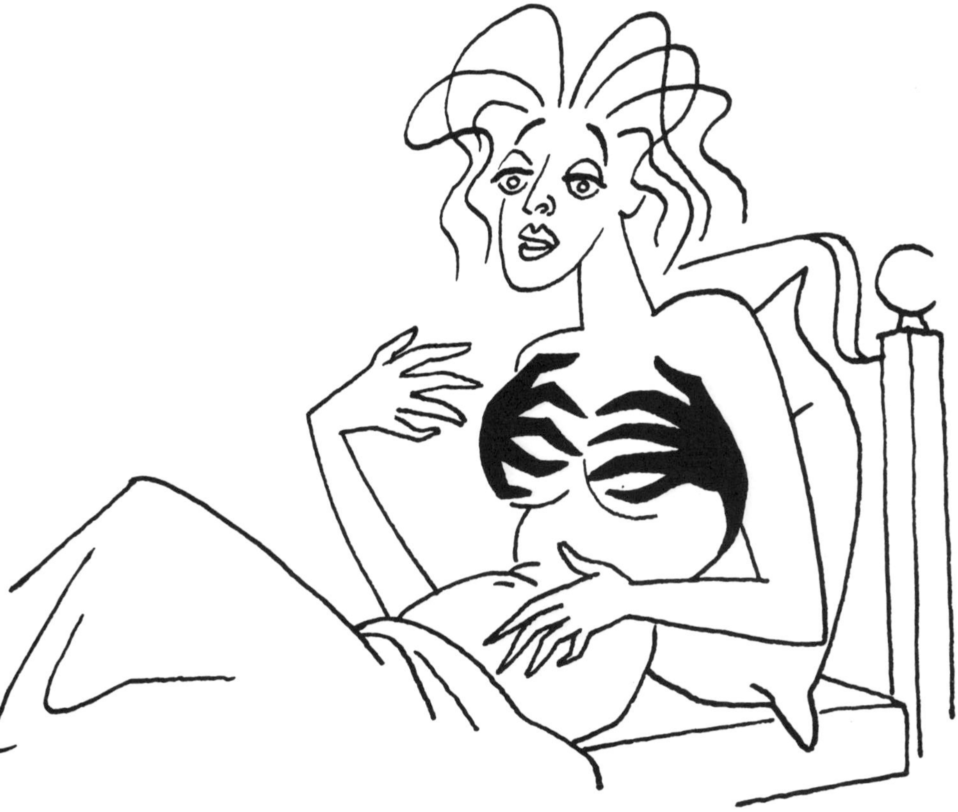

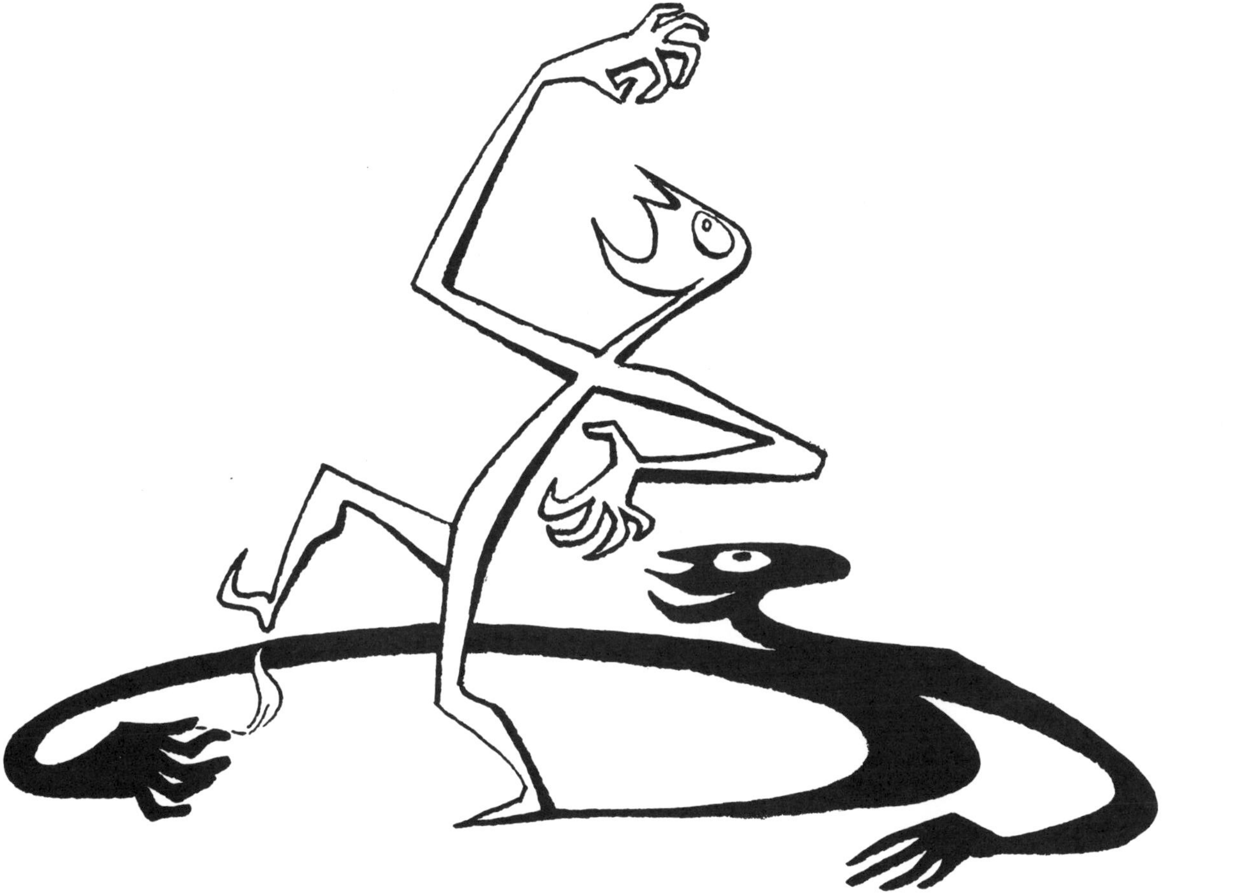

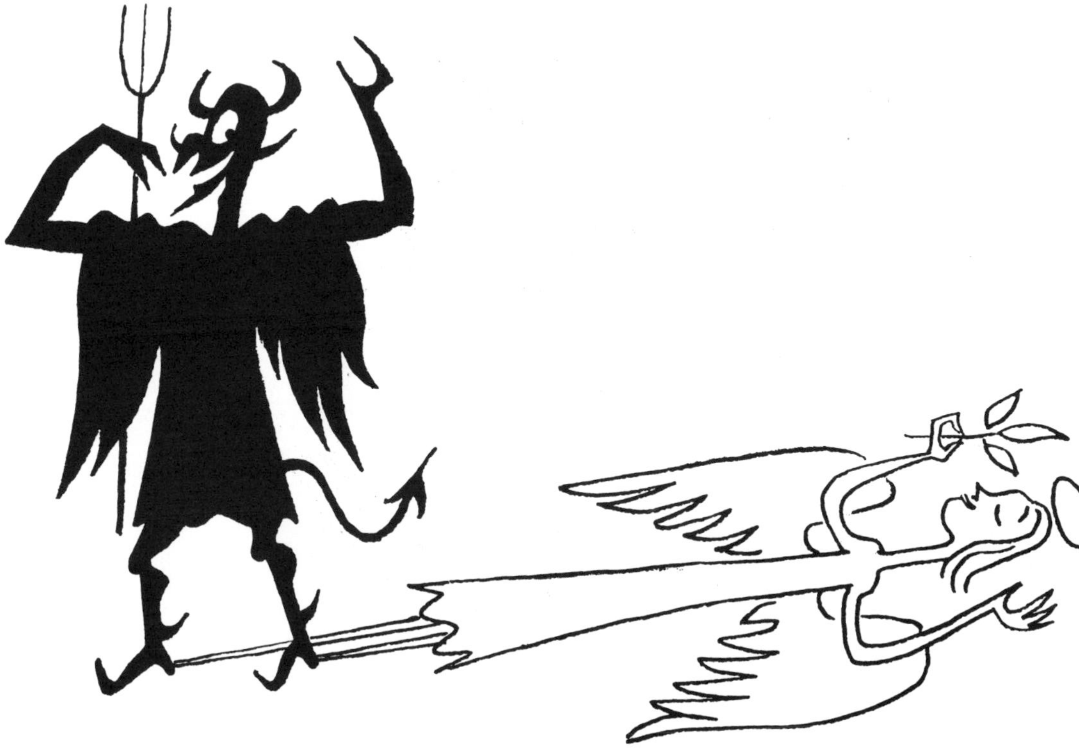

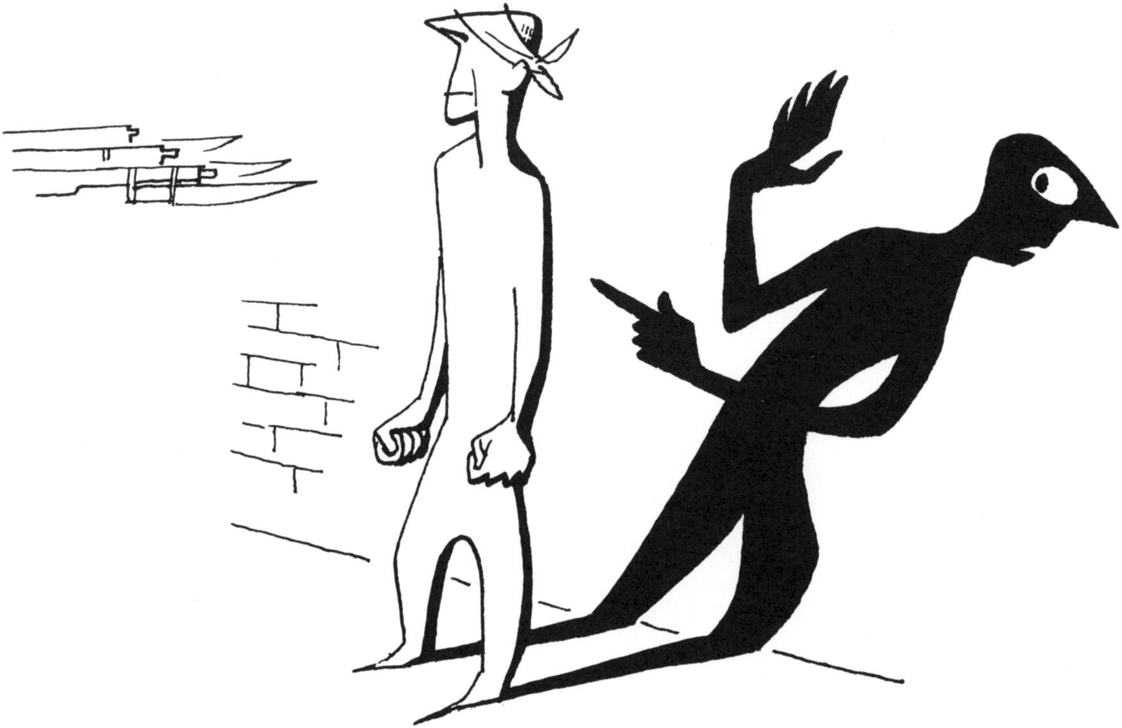

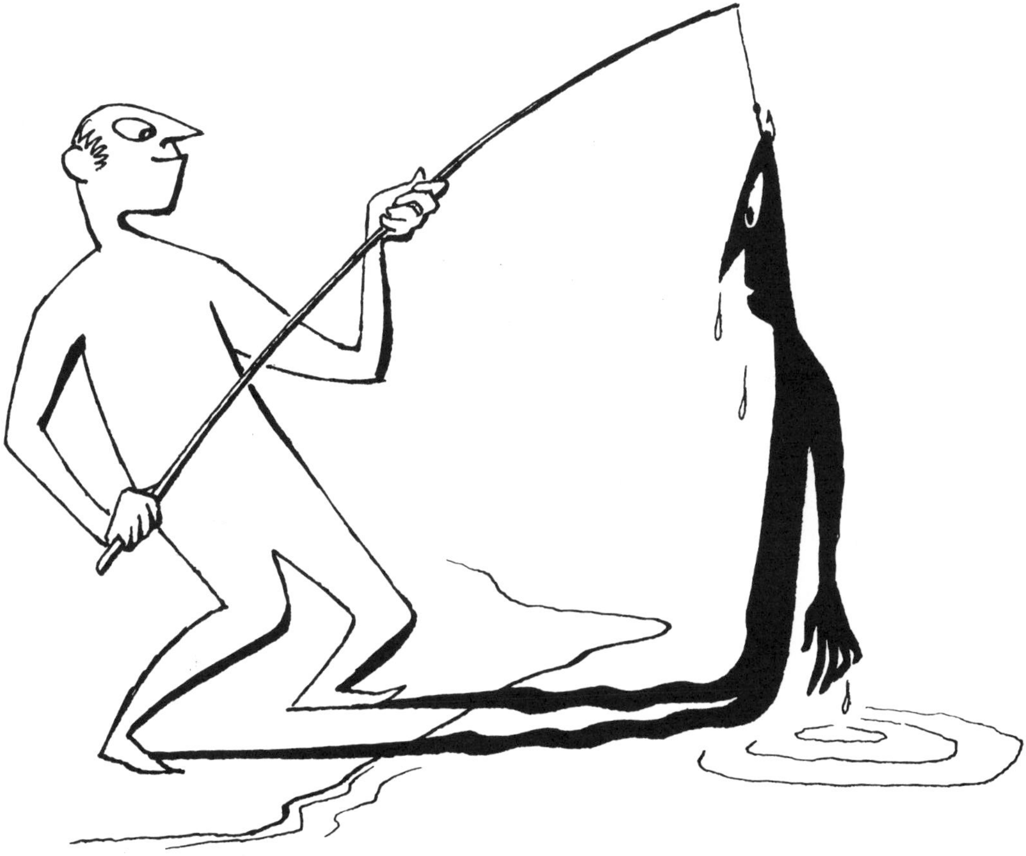

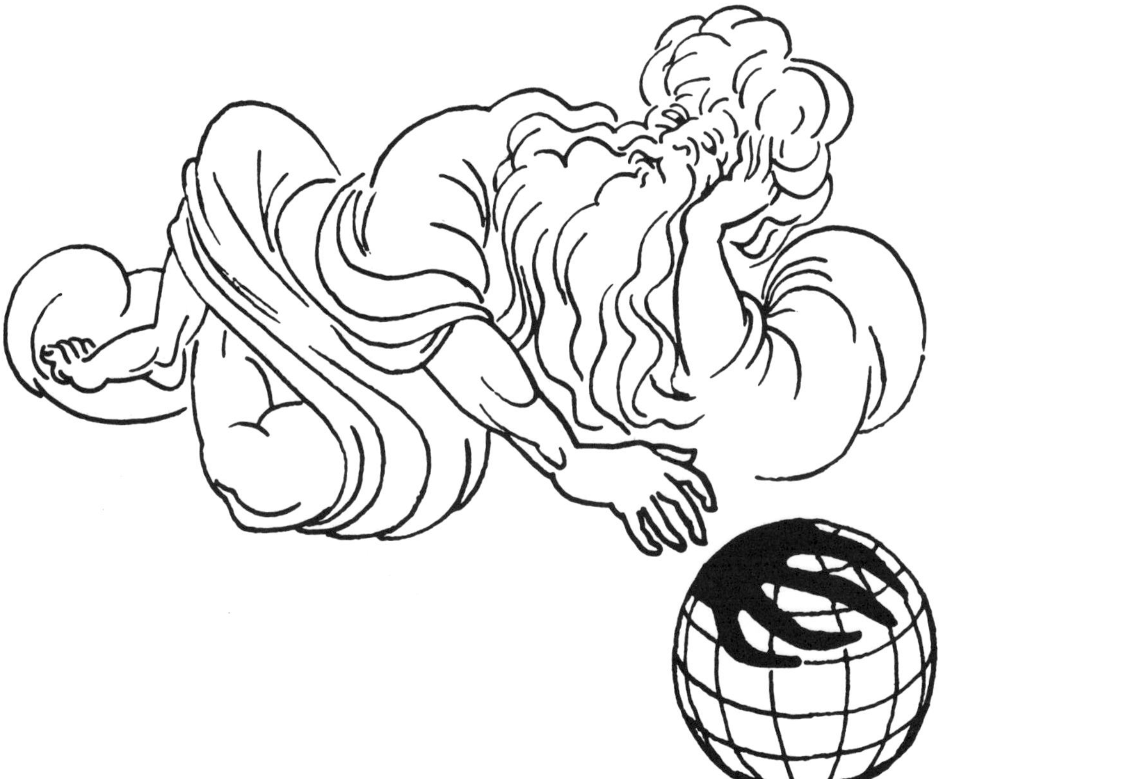

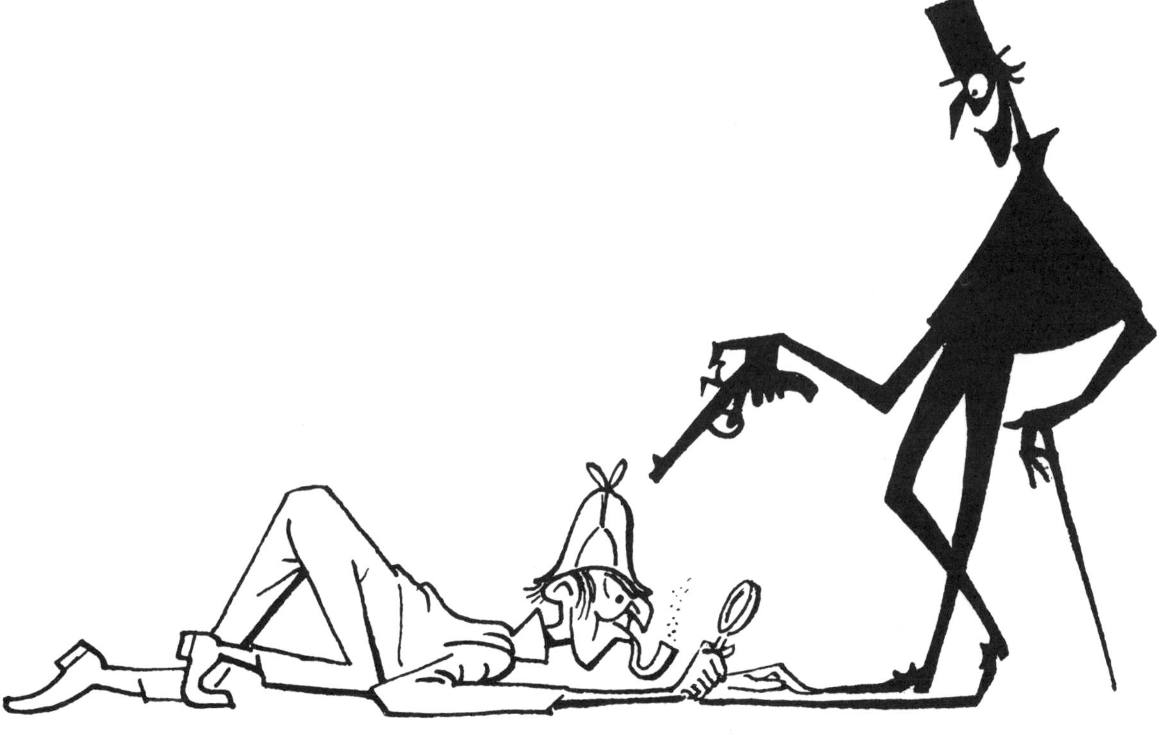

Pot Pour Rire

The following are random spot drawings
done by Harry between the 1950s
and 1990s.

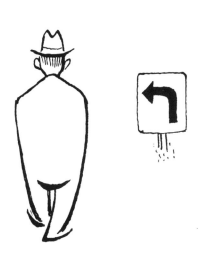

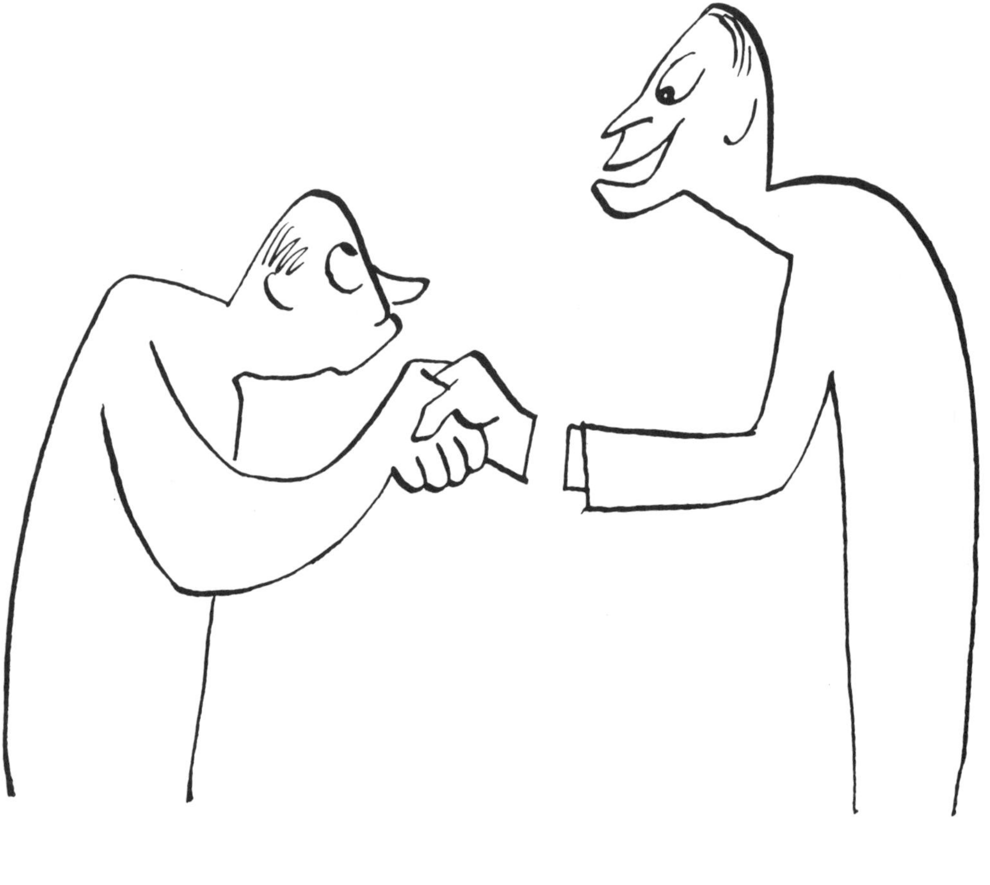

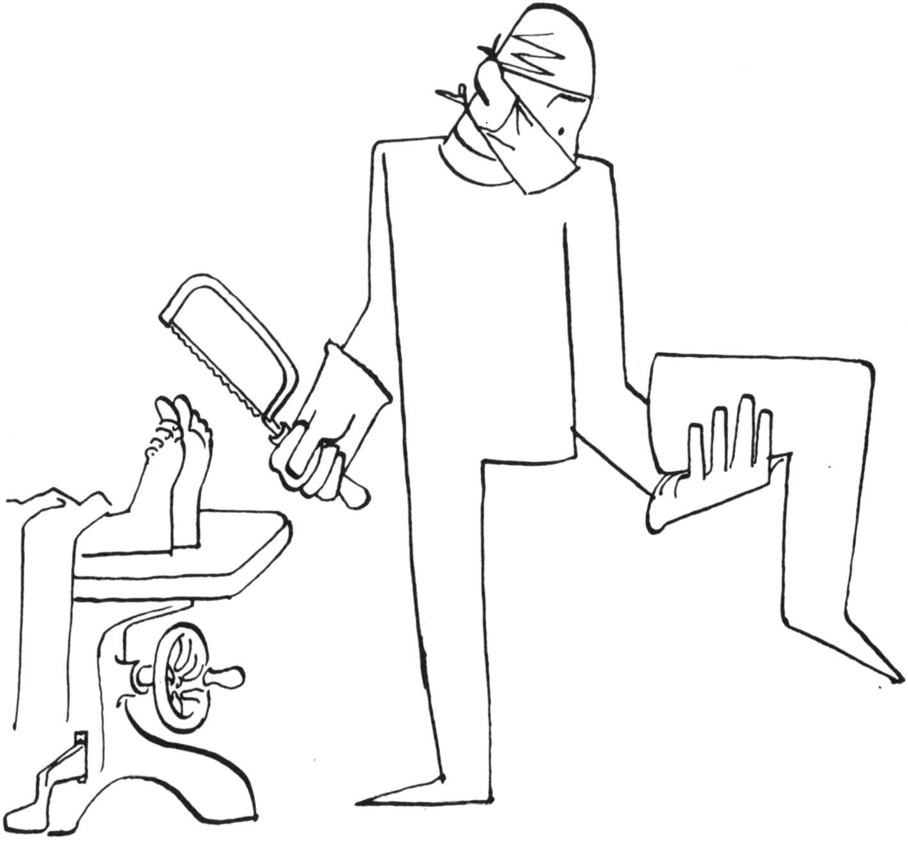

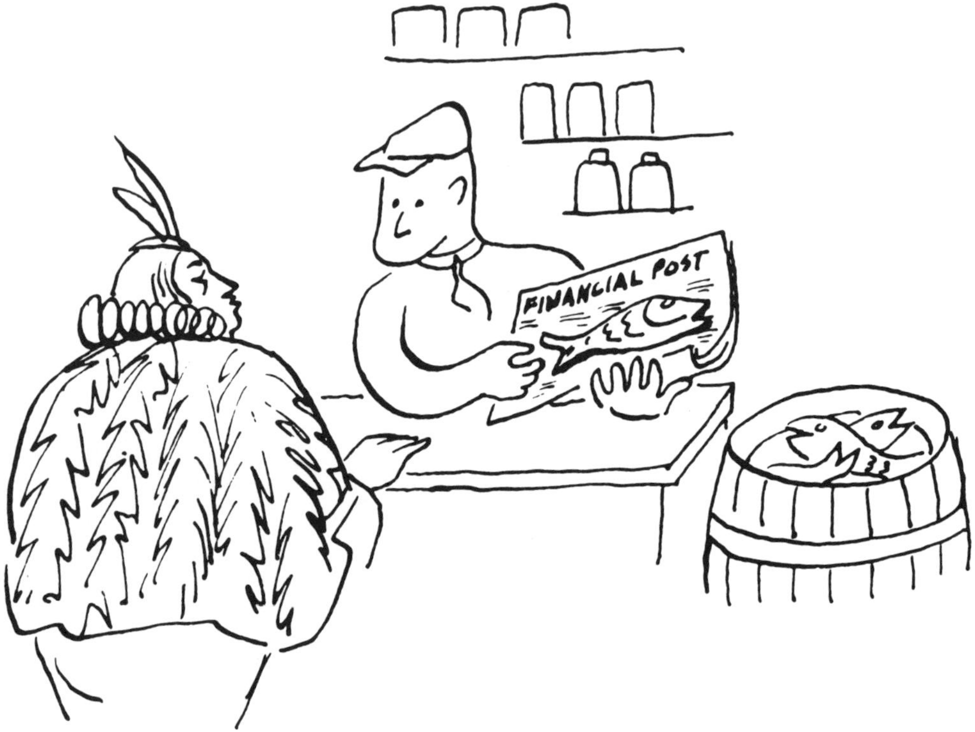
FINANCIAL POST

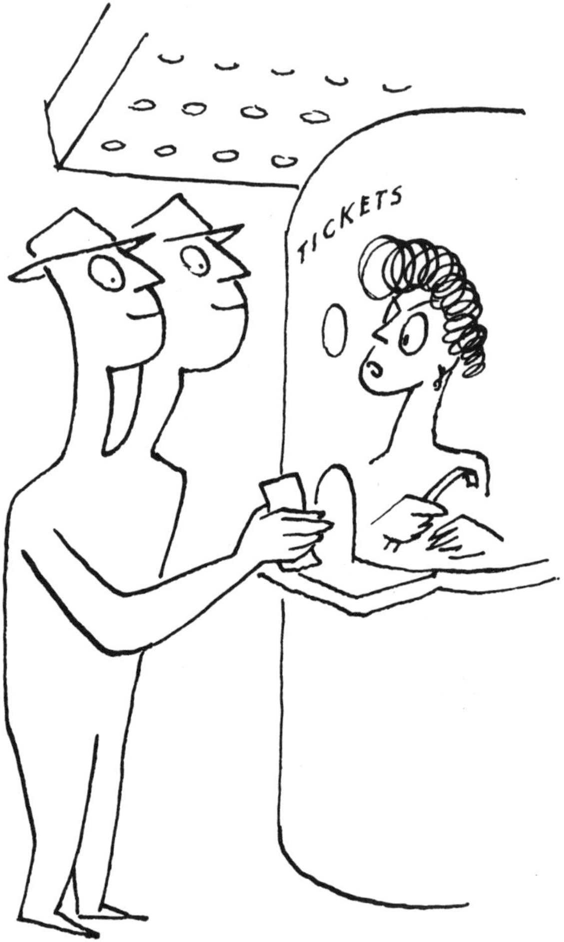
TICKETS

Way To Go

Drawings from 2002—2003.

"When you gotta go—YOU GOTTA GO! Que sera, sera. We are all destined to leap into the Great Beyond.

So why not go in style—with panache—with pizzazz? You may have messed up your life— failed to realize even your humblest fantasies. Don't despair. Make up for it on your way out. Grasp your big opportunity and depart in the glory! glory! glory! you have always aspired to. Make the nearest exit your Grande Finale! Who says 'you can't take it with you'?

Your destination? Who knows? Who cares? The fun is in getting there. So let me help you find a WAY-TO-GO. Why not, I ask you?"

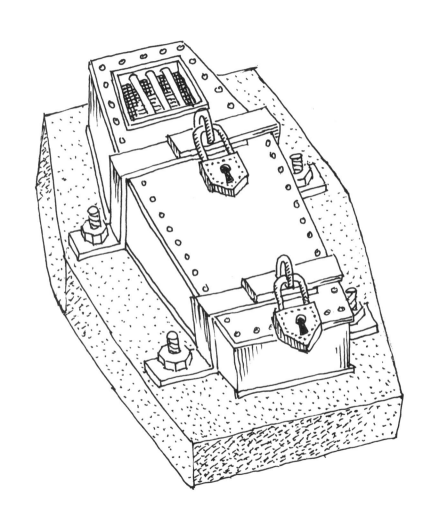

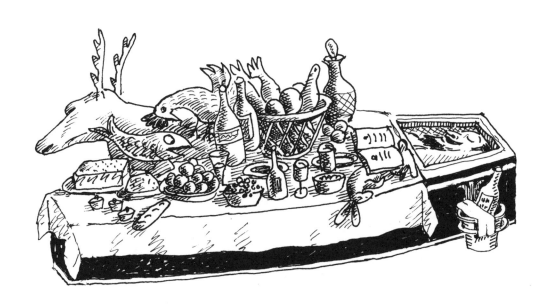

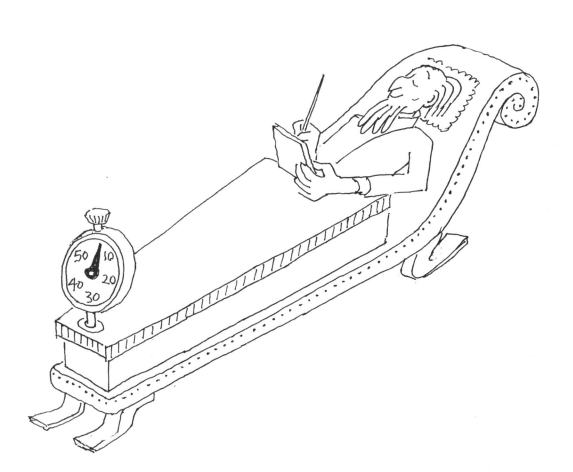

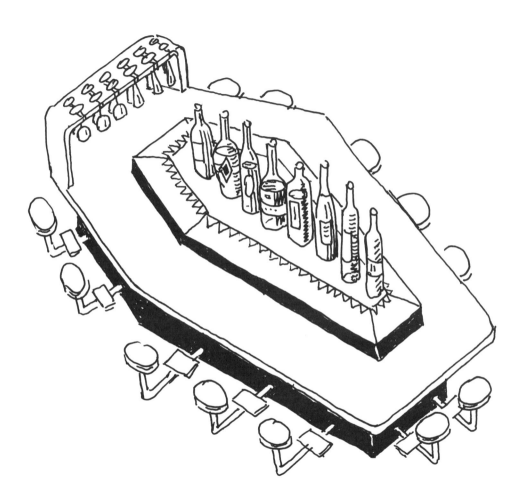

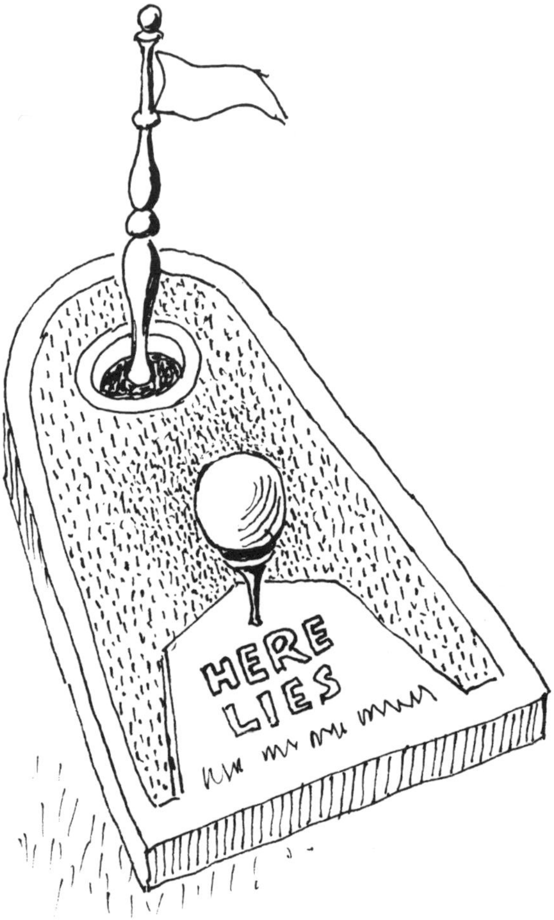
HERE
LIES

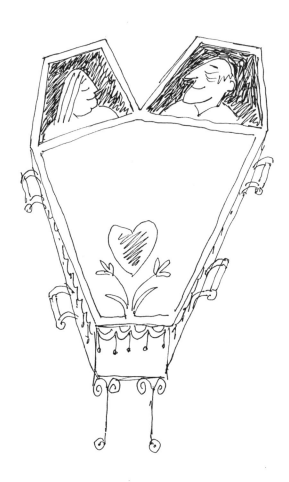

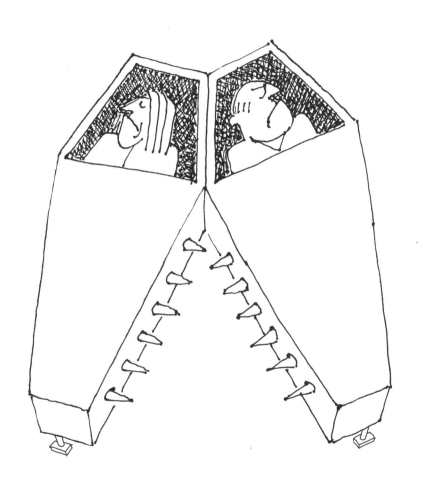

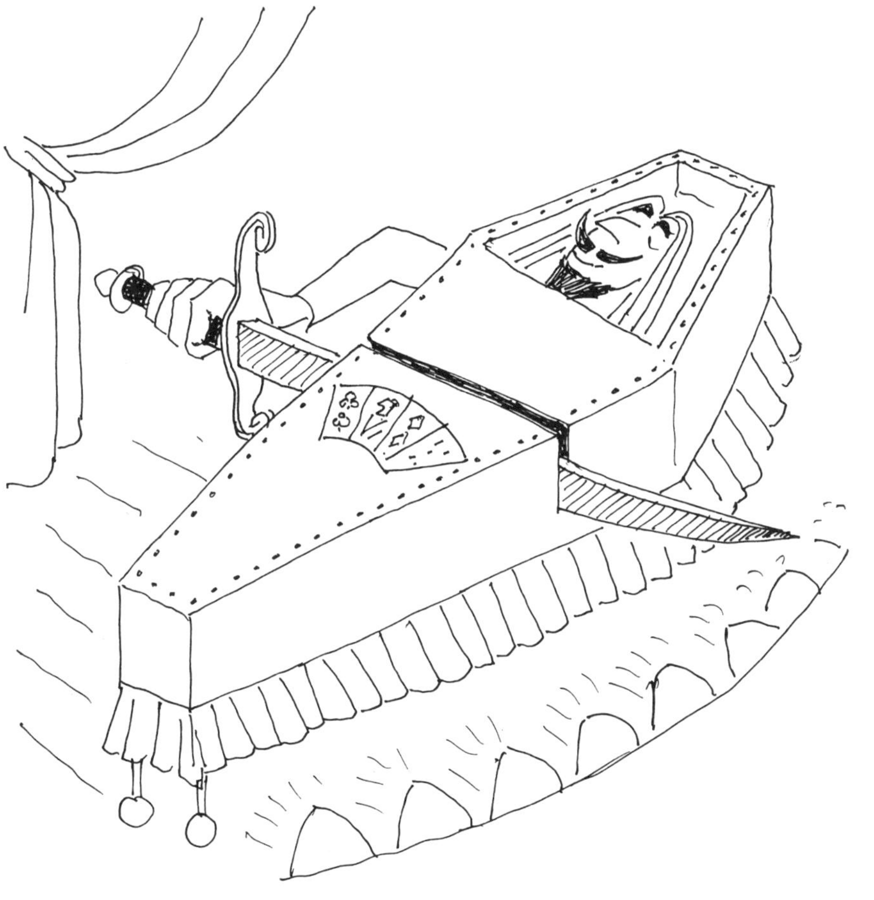

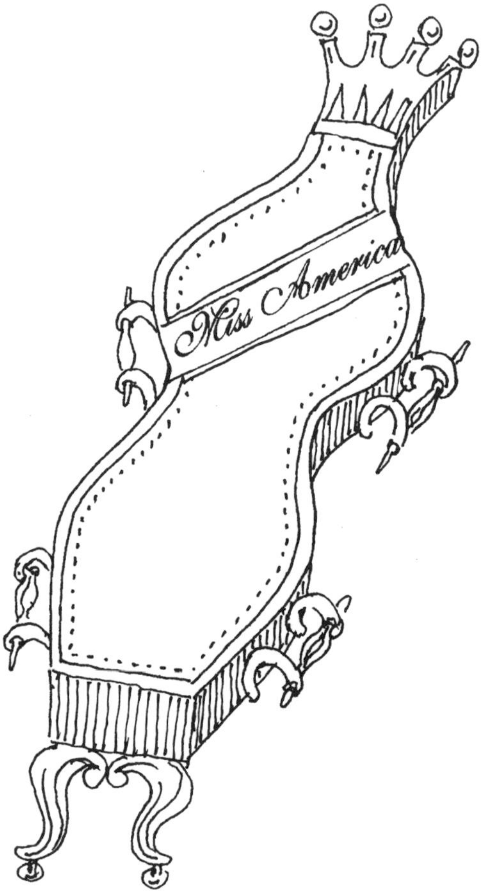
Miss America

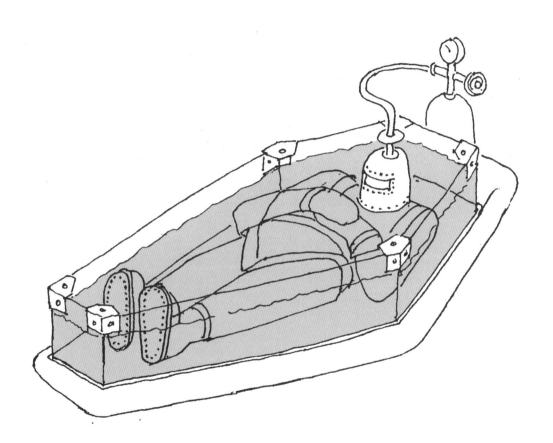

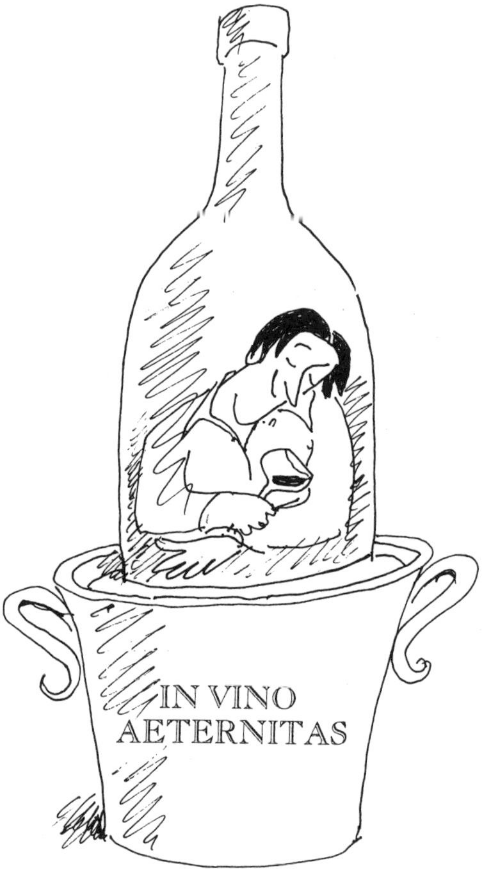
IN VINO
AETERNITAS

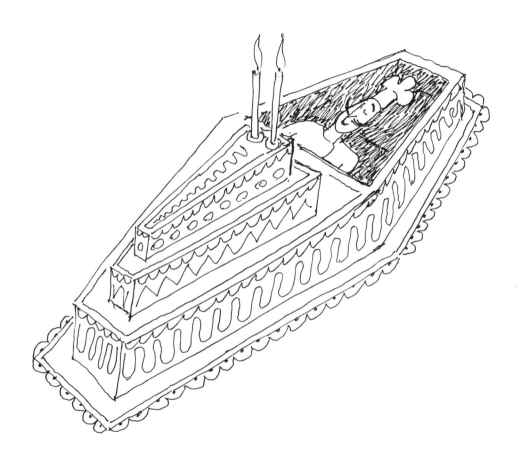

Harry Mayerovitch was born in Montreal in 1910 and has had a distinguished and varied career spanning most of the twentieth century. After graduating from McGill University in 1929, he worked as an architect, graphic designer, town planner, teacher, cartoonist, and painter for the next seven decades. His World War Two poster designs for the Canadian war effort are highly regarded and were recently featured in the pages of *Drawn & Quarterly*. His paintings and drawings are in the collections of The National Gallery of Canada, The Musée du Québec, The Montreal Museum of Fine Arts, and The National Portrait Gallery of Canada. Harry lives in Montreal where he continues to write, draw, and paint.